WORDSPINNING

OXFORD
UNIVERSITY PRESS

Great Clarendon Street, Oxford OX2 6DP

Oxford University Press is a department of the University of Oxford.
It furthers the University's objective of excellence in research, scholarship,
and education by publishing worldwide in

Oxford New York

Auckland Bangkok Buenos Aires Cape Town Chennai
Dar es Salaam Delhi Hong Kong Istanbul
Karachi Kolkata Kuala Lumpur Madrid Melbourne Mexico City
Mumbai Nairobi São Paulo Shanghai Taipei Tokyo Toronto

Oxford is a registered trade mark of Oxford University Press
in the UK and in certain other countries

British Library Cataloguing in Publication Data available

ISBN 0-19-276311 3

3 5 7 9 10 8 6 4 2

Typeset by Mary Tudge (Typesetting Services)

Design by Danny McBride

Printed in Great Britain
by Cox & Wyman Ltd, Reading, Berkshire

WORDSPINNING

Poems
collected by John Foster

Illustrated by
Mique Moriuchi

OXFORD
UNIVERSITY PRESS

Contents

Defending the Title

I am the word juggler.
I juggle the words
like swords.
I slice sense
with poetic licence.

I am the letter mover
the metre lover.
Like rhyme
I time this
for poetic justice.

I am the brain rattler.
Shaking ideas
like dice.
A notion
in poetic motion.

I am the verse-making
rule-bending defender.
Beginner
and ender.
I am the poet king.

Rachel Rooney

The Poetry Grand National

The poems line up
They're under starter's orders
They're off

Adverb leaps gracefully over the first fence
Followed by Adjective
A sleek, grey poem

Simile is overtaking on the outside
Like a pebble skimming the water

Halfway round the course
And Hyperbole is gaining on the leaders
Travelling at a million miles an hour

Adverb strides smoothly into first place

Haiku had good odds
But is far behind—and falls
At the last sylla-
ble

And as they flash past the winning post
The crowd are cheering
The winner is
Metaphor
Who quietly takes a bow

Roger Stevens

Acrostic

A cross tick
Could mean wrong answer, or
Right, if it is a correct, but cross, tick.
Or, if it is the tick of a clock,
Someone made the clock's tick tock
Tick
Into a
Cross tick.

Brenda Williams

I've Been Playing With Words

I've been playing with words.

I threw CATCH into the air—
And dropped it.
I've kicked the LL out of BALL
(Which has left me with BA).
I've wiped the floor with MOP
And I've given STOMACH a good prod.
I've sat on CUSHION
And MARBLE has just rolled under the sofa.

Mum says that LOUNGE isn't for lazing
And that I've made it look a right MESS.

So I've got to collect up
All the words again
And put them away—*tidily*—
In my Dictionary.

Before Dad gets home.

Trevor Harvey

Knitted Scarf Poem

Note: This poem has been knitted, so of course, you must start at the bottom and work up.

I dropped a s
Till carelesslyt
Without a hitchi
To make an odet
Then one row plainc
First one row purlh
With might and main
I knitted long
Scarf of verse
A thick and warming
And ball of words
With size six pins
A poem scarf
I thought I'll knit
So for a laugh
The day was cold

George Moore

10

*Shoem

Time flizzes when I'm wrizzing—
some words are toomely long,
and so I merge and jummix
to squeet them in my song.

It's really not too diffcky
to get my words to scrush—
saves tromoil and timassle,
when in a hurrid rush.

There's only one small difflem
for my puzzizzy head—
I'm baffplussed and conboozled
by what it is I said!

*Short Poem

Flizzes = flies and whizzes
Wrizzing = busy and writing
Toomely = too and extremely
Jummix = jumble and mix
Squeet = squeeze and fit
Diffcky = difficult and tricky
Scrush = squash and crush
Tromoil = trouble and turmoil
Timassle = time and hassle
Hurrid = hurried and horrid
Difflem = difficulty and problem
Puzzizzy = puzzled and dizzy
Baffplussed = baffled and nonplussed
Conboozled = confused and bamboozled

Liz Brownlee

Anagrimes

Live to evil, veil to vile;
And leap to plea to peal to pale;
Dear, read, and dare; then lime and mile.
From late to teal and on to tale.

Shop, posh, and hops; from Rome to more.
From tame to team to meat to mate.
Turn gnat to tang. Turn horse to shore.
Move tape to peat and on to pate.

Shift leaf to flea. Slide lids to slid.
Change nuts to stun and kids to skid.
Switch Eros into sore or rose,
And hose to shoe or same-sound hoes.

Twist stub to buts to tubs to bust.
Swing Mars to arms and loot to tool.
Mix stop and tops and spots and post.
Drive rats to star and loop to pool.

The anagram spins round and round.
It plays with spelling; plays with sound.
In this long list I've given you,
There's still a missing word or—two!

Where would you fit 'rams' and 'polo'? Have I missed any more?

John Kitching

12

Spelling Riddles

A vocal ruby
Is your wordstore.

Toes in evil
Will give you square eyes.

Dice moan—
And the rest laugh.

The plane
Is a vast creature.

Ken glowed
As he knew so much.

Foes rant on
Always after twelve.

O pity slim ibis
For this cannot be done.

Pie Corbett

Music Riddle—What Am I?

My first is in **racket** which some say I cause
My second's in **clap** and also **applause**
My third is in **record** and twice can be found
Whilst my fourth is in **cassette** but never in sound
My fifth hides in **pop** and also in **song**
My sixth is in **soundtrack** to help you along
My last is in **tune** and **singer** and **stage**
What could I be? I'm now all the rage.

Richard Caley

Answer: KARAOKE

Riddle

We ride on weapons
mightier than swords.
Make peace but
sign lives away.
Used to extremes
we keep up to scratch.
In honour of service
are given rings
but can be rude
when it comes to the point.

John C. Desmond

Hide and Seek Words

Somewh<u>re in</u> these sentences
there are hidden words
that have their beginning
in one word and
their end in the next word.

Look carefully
and you will notice
that there are
quite a mixture
of words to pick from,
so pay close attention
to the appearance
of the alphabet.

The tiger
ate a goat
before stopping
by the village
to escape
the people
that were
struggling round.

Pie Corbett

16

A Parrot

J. Patrick Lewis

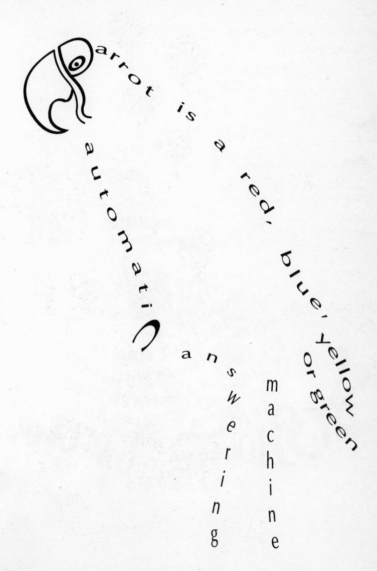

Parrot is a red, blue, yellow or green automatic answering machine

This Snail

Jenny Morris

THIS
SNAIL
HIDES IN
ITS SHELL
AND HOPES NO
ONE CAN TELL
THAT IT'S INSIDE
IN FEAR
WHENEVER DANGER'S NEAR
IT BUBBLES OUT SOME FROTH
TO FRIGHTEN THRUSHES OFF
ITS TENTACLES HAVE EYES
IT GLIDES ROUND IN DISGUISE
JUST LIKE A
SPIRAL STONE
ITS HOUSE IS ALL HOMEGROWN

The Spelling Spell

(A Phonic Tonic)

Put my **i**s before my **e**s.
Twist them round when after **c**s.
Sort my **ort**s and **aught**s and **ough**ts
(And what about the **ort** in wart?)
Put my **ite**s and **ight**s to right
Add the sneaky **k** to knight.
Check **ee**s and **ea**s and add a **u**
Every time I form a **q**.
Grab bossy **e**s that spit with spite
Add **w**s to wrong and write.
Don't forget the **ool**s and **ule**s
And foolish ghouls that break the rules.
Then, if that isn't quite enough
Separate my **uff**s from **ough**s.
Choose the proper kind of **oo**
In crews that cruise the blues with you.
Then dot my **i**s and cross my **t**s
And get my spelling test right—PLEASE!

Maureen Haselhurst

English as a Foreign Language

sea as in ocean
see with your eyes
eight follows seven
ate as in pies
threw as in chucked it
through means go through
jeans are for wearing
genes make you YOU
bare means no clothes on
bear is a beast
fair can mean playground
fare can mean feast
two is a number
too means as well
peel is a fruit skin
peal as in bell
where? is a question
wear means have on
passed as in gave it
past means it's gone
nit is a head louse
knit things with wool
rain as in brollies up
reign means to rule
knight clad in armour
night follows day
son meaning offspring
sun golden rays
ball which you play with
bawl is to cry
site means location

sight as in eye
hare like a rabbit
hair on your head
dye is to colour
die as in dead
might meaning power
mite a small bug
pore is an opening
pour from a jug.

In English words may sound alike
But differ in allusion
The way we spell them differs too
Which adds to our confusion.

I've tried to highlight some of these
Two more are **lone** and **loan**
These ever so confusing words
Are known as homophones.

Richard Caley

Beware of Silent Letters

Beware of silent letters
That creep up unannounced,
Insisting that they should be spelt
Though never once pronounced.

Like solemn ghosts from mouldy tombs
They subtly haunt our words,
And act like model children
Who are seen but never heard.

We'd like to wring their wretched necks
But sadly lack the knack
Of harming those who will not fight
Or even answer back.

And so they stay to plague us,
As troublesome as gnats,
Swarming across our written words
And infiltrating chats.

So beware of silent letters
For you'll find them everywhere,
Sneaking up on their verbal prey
In a way that's most unfair.

Cynthia Rider

U Knee Verse

A stacks are good to sleep in
B troot sandwiches are yuck
C d looking bloke
D sent looking bloke
E did it, not me
F only I hadn't got caught
G knee us
H l o is larger than a violin
I for an i
J l him for life
K tering for all tastes
L bow grease
M barrassed by my spots
N joyed the party
O pless at spellin
P pol keep staring at me
Q er ring my bad habits is impossible
R you sure it was him
S a was due in yesterday
T tering on the brink
U knee verse
V nus and Mars bars
W up with pain
X hausted by trying to work this out
Y me
Z too much and had to sit in silence

David Kitchen

The Monsters of Loch Ness

There's Bold Ness the brave
And Dull Ness the boring
Dark Ness the gloomy
And Fierce Ness the roaring
There's Shy Ness the bashful
Nasty Ness the bad
Glad Ness the cheerful
And Grim Ness the sad
There's Happy Ness the joyful
And Tough Ness the hardy
Lazy Ness the idle
And Late Ness the tardy
There's Smart Ness the dapper
Tidy Ness the neat
There's Kind Ness the gentle
And Cute Ness the sweet
There's Calm Ness the tranquil

And Thin Ness the slender
Rough Ness the bully
And Good Ness the tender
There's Dirty Ness the filthy
Rebellious Ness the defiant
Clumsy Ness the awkward
And Huge Ness the giant
There's Pure Ness the wholesome
And Quick Ness the speedy
Plump Ness the podgy
And Small Ness the weedy
There's Nervous Ness the worried
And Pleasant Ness the charming
Petty Ness the spiteful
And Loud Ness the alarming
They're lurking there now
In the depths of Loch Ness
Avoiding the cameras
With effortlessness.

Granville Lawson

Song of the Aitch

'Huh!' is the sound an aitch makes
At the start of many a word,
But in the word for 'H' itself
That sound is never heard.

Try looking in your dictionary
Under 'H' for HAITCH,
And you will never find it
Cos it's under 'A' for Aitch.

So many people drop them
(Particularly in France),
But you should never do so
Under any circumstance.

Words like 'Happy hairy hamsters'
All start with H's letter,
But 'Aitch' has got one at the end.
Remember that! You'd better!

Pam Gidney

Accents

My little Northern cousin, Cath,
Each evening loves to have a bath.
When in the South with brother Garth,
Does little Cathy have a bath?

John Kitching

The Boy Who Mislaid His Vowels (inc. 'y') Writes a Note to his Teacher

Pls xcs m , hv lst ll m vwls.
 thnk   lft thm n th bs
 t ws nmbr 68 (thnk)
M mthr s vr pst
M dd thmpd m
M sstr jst lghd
Th gldfsh s nhpp
Th ct wnt t ts Whsks
 dnt knw wht   cn d
 wll tr t fnd thm ltr
 hv dn m ggrph hmwrk
 nd m mths
 nd m scnc
 nd m hstr
Cn hv sm mr vwls pls ?
Pls xcs m . m vr vr srr .

Peter Mortimer

Low Owl

—a univolic*

Cold morn: on fork of two o'clock
owl's hoot flows from hood of wood.

Owl's song rolls from blood to brood,
owl's hoot loops onto top of town roofs,
owl's song swoops on strong doors.

Owl's slow whoop—long, forlorn—
soft flood of moon song.

John Rice

*a poem which uses only one of the five vowels: in this case the letter 'o'.

Never Odd or Even

My teacher, Miss Hannah Stillits,
collects palindromes.

She started when
she was just a **bab**;
mum and **dad** were her first.
Then some other easy ones,
like **pip** and **pop**.

But it wasn't long before
Hannah got mobile with
racecar and **kayak**,
and toilet-trained
with **gnu dung**.

When she went to school,
her teacher was a **nun** who
loved old cats (**senile felines**),
'**Step on no pets**,' said the **nun**.

Young Hannah's best friend was **Evil Olive**.
Olive had an owl, but it was
too hot to hoot.

'**Dammit I'm mad**,' said **Evil Olive** one day.
'**Mr Owl ate my metal worm**. A wicked **deed**.'
'Then **live not on evil, madam, live not on evil**,' said the **nun**.
'**We few** must reach the **top spot**, mustn't we?'
The children nodded.
'**Don't nod**,' said the **nun**.

Hannah collected
all the palindromes she could.
As a teenager, she wondered
Do geese see god?
And once, she fell into
a *party trap*; or was it
a *party boobytrap*?

And so, Miss Hannah *Stillits*
went to college and became
a teacher.

I learned that
rats live on no evil star
she said. But
was it a bar or a bat I saw?
Was it a car or a cat I saw?

'It was a *ewe*,' we told her.
'Oh, *I did, did I*?' she said sleepily.
'I must learn to
yawn a more Roman way.'
And she fell asleep at *noon*.
ZzzzzzzzzzzzzzzzzzzzzzzzzzzzzZ

Mike Jubb

The Missing Vowel

Can you spy
By your teeny eye
The naughty vowel
That passed me by?

John Kitching

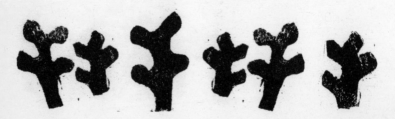

Plurules

1. Two fives are ten but two man is men
2. A solitary geese is a goose but a lonely moose is still a moose
3. One children is a child and one lice is just a louse
   Cod and his friends are cod but a single mice's a mouse
4. The giraffes' hoofs rang out on the roofs
   However
   The elves put up shelves themselves
5. Stratum plus stratum equals strata
   Datum plus datum equals data

   And remember

6. Trousers, breeches, pants cannot be worn
   In their singular form.

Petonelle Archer

Rhinos and Roses

Gina Douthwaite

When more than one rhinoceros
becomes rhinoceroses, and each of these
has horns of hair that stick up from their
noses, and armoured skin that wallows in
the mud when they reposes, and on each
foot each rhino has three hooves
instead of toeses – the features
of these creatures show
the problem language poses
when more
than one
rhino-
ceros

be-
comes
rhinoc-
eroses.

Teachers Named and Shamed

Miss Isles—Got a rocket and went off somewhere.
Mister Boat—Didn't come back from his holidays.
Miss Fire—Went off too soon.
Miss T. Day—Got lost in the fog.
Miss Led—Joined a heavy metal rock band.
Miss Demeanour—Was sent to prison.
Miss Cue—Married Mister Black and went to live in Poole.
Miss Spell—Lepht in dizgrase.
Mister Penalty—Resigned and became a professional footballer.
Miss Laid—Got lost.
Miss Hap—Went to live with Miss Adventure.
Miss Understood—Is still teaching in the school;
   we can't understand it.

David Whitehead

School Reports

Di Version	Likes to go her own sweet way
Peter Out	Always tired by end of day
Penny Coyne	One in a hundred, but won't go far
Stella Nova	A very bright star
A. Lian	Not like the rest
Maxi Mumme	Tries to give his best
Ella Vator	Sometimes up, sometimes down
Micky Taker	Likes to act the classroom clown
A. Loner	Rarely mixes with the mass
Gerry Atrick	Somewhat old for this young class
Mo Bility	An active child who sets good pace
Den Tist	The sort who's always 'in your face'
Rhoda Way	Often absent from the school
Jack Daw	A bird-brained child who acts the fool
Vi Tality	Here's a girl who's full of life
Etty Quette	So well mannered and polite

Hugh Jeffort	Tries so hard to give his all
Minnie Mumme	Never works, won't try at all
Billy Ards	He's right on cue
Reece Ikle	Like last term—nothing new
Ivor Packett	Spends his time with Robin Banks
Tim Burr	Thick as two planks
Hugo First	Who hates to lead
Fred Bare	A child in need?
Honey Combe	Well *behived* and rather sweet
Dilly Gent	Thorough worker, very neat
Stan Dalone	Just won't join in
Vic Tory	Likes to win
Orson Cart	Just plods along
Polly Filler	Sticks at task and very strong
Cliff Edge	I think he's heading for a fall
Robin Banks	Always has the wherewithal

Brenda Williams

Saintly Poems

St Able houses
clever horses.
St Ale lets
the beer turn flat.
St Rain keeps us
trying if it pours.

St Ark sets sail
when it is bleak.
St Eel may wriggle
but is hard.
St Ate is well fed
in the country.

And St One
is singular
but breaks bones.

Pie Corbett

More Saintly Poems

St Art is a beginner
who is learning how to draw.

St Rip is a tearaway
who dresses in football kit.

St Rum is a guitar-player
who plays odd tunes.

St Rap is a hanger-on
with fingers snapping
and feet tap-tapping.

And St Ill is a patient
lying in hospital, motionless.

John Foster

Won, Too, Free

Won is the race that you ran and came first,
Too is as well or much more than enough,
Free costs you nothing, not being locked up,
Fore's to the front and a warning in golf,
'F I've not got one then neither shall you,
Sick's what you are when you've eaten too much,
'S heaven to lie on a tropical beach,
Ate's what you did to the grub on your plate,
'Nein' say the Germans who aren't saying yes,
Tense—the feeling you get when you're stressed.

Trevor Parsons

A Mathematician's Love Song

I 1der, would it be 2 much,
Too footloose and too fancy 3,
4 our short friendship to sur5
A trip to Su6, by the sea?
We'd walk the 7 Sisters cliffs,
And contempl8 the peaceful view,
And stroll be9ly down forgo10
Country lanes, just me and you.

Julia Rawlinson

Dr D. Rision's Shopping List

scornflakes
laughing stock cubes
sour grapes
caustic soda
scathing pads
marshmalice
acid drops
throat sweets (honey and venom)
spite bulbs (40 watt)
ginger jeer
teasebags
Taunt-on cider
mock turtle soup
fault and pepper
Cornish nasty
crabby paste
carp
I can't Believe it's not Bitter!
1 pkt choccy takethemickeys
baked spleens
bread (Mother's Snide)
disdain remover
scoff for dinner party
gripe water

Sue Cowling

@

I am a sign whose time has come.
Sign of the times, I'm where it's @,
a stylish techn-aristocr@.
In all e-mails, to each dot com,

though no bigger than gn@ or crumb
or b@'s left thumb, the truth is th@
I am a sign whose time has come.
Sign of the times, I'm where it's @.

I am, you see, from this time on,
not just the rhyme in c@, m@, s@—
it's me you need for on-line ch@.

The web is where I'm coming from.
I am a sign whose time has come.
Sign of the times, I'm where it's @.

David Horner

Missing

MISSING
HAVE YOU SEEN THIS DOT?
·
small black answers to
Dot or Full Stop
Disappeared last Friday
Dotnapped?
? and ! both pining
e-mail desperate
contact KEYBOARD WATCH
to earn cash reward

Sue Cowling

Dads Views' on Apostrophe's

Apostrophe's often appear in place's
where they are not mean't to,
like in grocery shop's windows'
advertising orange's and apple's,
or they are omitted when they shouldnt be.
Its all very confusing, isnt it?
Dad say's if hed got any say
(which he hasnt)
hed abolish the bloomin thing's.

John Foster

Commas

Commas like, apostrophes
often, appear in places
where, they shouldn't,
But Dad, says
they are a different,
kettle of fish,
you need, to know
how to use, them properly,
you shouldn't, just scatter them,
everywhere like, confetti,

John Foster

Semi Colon

I feel sorry for the ;
it doesn't do a lot
it's just a little comma
with a silly little dot.
I'd like to use it often
but I don't know
      really how
. . . so I'll pop some
      in this poem
Look! Here come semis now ; ; ;

Peter Dixon

Smith, Hacket, and Grimes

I cannot say, with hand on heart,
I care for Mr Smith:
A preposition he will use
To end a sentence with.

And neither do I like a lot
Someone called Mrs Hacket.
(She puts things in parenthesis
And doesn't close the bracket.

But I can scarce put into words
How much I hate Miss Grimes.
She wants to be a poetess,
But writes appalling verses.

Colin West

Corrections

Teacher said,
Leave out the the,
two too's one too too many
and and after the comma
should go after the any.

The the, the too—
and move the and
and that should make it flow.
Not that that, that that's fine—
but this that, that could go.

I said,
The the, the too, the and—
I would agree with you.
But I'm very fond of that—
this that and that that too.

Which that is that?
Is that this that?
Asked teacher with a grin.
OK—but take that last in out
And leave that last out in.

Roger Stevens

More Metaphor

There are fleas in our ears,
And frogs in our throats.
We've got ants in our pants.
We're burning our boats.

With bees in our bonnets,
There's pie in the sky.
When we've kicked the bucket,
We'll see eye to eye.

Curiosity's killed
The old kitchen cat.
It's raining just dogs.
Who'd ever think that?

John Kitching

How Can I?

How can I wind up my brother
when I haven't got the key?

How can I turn on my charm
when I can't even find the switch?

How can I snap at my mother
when I'm not a crocodile?

How can I stir up my sister
when I'm not even holding a spoon?

How can I pick up my feet
and not fall to the ground on my knees?

How can I stretch my legs
when they're long enough already?

Parents! They ask the impossible!

Brian Moses

My Hypochondriac Kitchen

The freezer complains of chilblains,
and the whole kitchen starts feeling sorry for itself.

The carpet is depressed.
'It's like I'm getting under everyone's feet.'
'I feel washed out,' says the dishcloth.
'I'm put upon all the time,' adds a shelf.
'I can't take the strain any more,' sobs the colander.
The coffee machine sighs, 'I used to be so full of beans.'
The radiator shivers, 'I just can't seem to get warm.'
'Me neither,' agrees the oven.
'I'm all blocked up,' moans the sink.
The kettle hisses, 'I've got an enormous boil.'
'I keep blowing hot and cold,' says the fan.
'My head's spinning,' groans the washing machine.

'Come on,' says the curtains,
'Pull yourselves together.'

John Coldwell

The Detestable Cliché

Oh, how I detest the cliché,
Which you know, at the end of the day,
To be honest just slips
Off everyone's lips
And the bottom line is, it's passé.

Cynthia Rider

The Complete Works of Father Christmas (So Far)

A Midwinter Night's Dream
As Cold As You Like It
Julius Freezer
Snowthello
Rudolph and Juliet
The Merry Elves of Windsor
The Winter's Trail
The Taming of the Flue
Sackbeth

The Merchant of Lapland
Much Ado About Shopping
The Comedy of Mixed-up Presents
Turkeyandhamlet
King Wenceslas (Part I and II)

Work in progress:
All's Well That Ends On Twelfth Night.

Sue Cowling

Smart Talk

Idioms are rather smart
For they never mean what they say,
Which you'd think would tend
To lead you a dance
And yet, by some amazing chance,
Instead of making you lose your thread,
They actually hit the nail on the head.

Cynthia Rider

Short Words

Short words that we use, such as *bee*, *bat*, or *bird*,
Go under a name quite inapt and absurd;
No wonder this adjective seldom is heard,
For *monosyllabic*, I fear, is the word.

Colin West

'Repeat After Me . . .'

At the 'Déjà Vu' School
Work is *always* the same;
If they've done it *before*,
They just *do it again*!

Trevor Harvey

Proverbial Fun

Half a loaf is better than last night's take-away.
A garlic a day, keeps everyone away.
The early bird teaches the worm to sleep late.
Where there's a will you're not intestate.
A bird in the hand will make a mess on your sleeve.
One man's meat makes another man heave.
Too many cooks make a lot of washing up.
Great oaks from little acorns take years to grow up.
He who laughs last is a bit slow on the uptake.
A rolling stone will sink in a lake.
When the cat's away, the dog has the rug.
You make your bed, so make it snug.

Brenda Williams

Well-Known Proverbs

H A N bird D = B U ₂ S H

H ♡ M E

WRONG
+ WRONG
―――――――――
NOT CORRECT

Paul Cookson

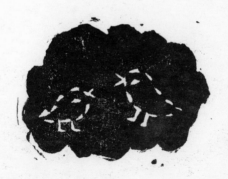

This Poem

This poem is made up
of 100 per cent recycled
words and, once read,
can be carefully
cut up and reused.

Michael Harrison

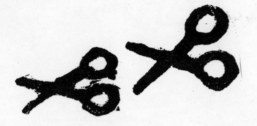

Hindsight

Yesterday
I went to get my hindsight tested.
It was perfect.
Looking back,
I should have known that.

Andy Seed

Done

F's in the traffic
I's in begin
N is for nothing
I is for in
S is for singing
H is for hum
E is for ending
D is for done

David Kitchen

Acknowledgements

We are grateful for permission to reproduce the following poems: **Liz Brownlee**: 'Shoem' © Liz Brownlee 2003, first published in *The Apple Raid* chosen by Pie Corbett (Macmillan), included by permission of the author; **Sue Cowling**: 'Dr D. Rision's Shopping List' © Sue Cowling 2001, first published in *The Evil Doctor Mucus Spleen* (Macmillan) and 'Missing' © Sue Cowling 2000, first published in *A Mean Fish Smile* (Macmillan), included by permission of the author; **Gina Douthwaite**: 'Rhinos and Roses' © Gina Douthwaite 2002 from *What Shape's an Ape?* (Red Fox) included by permission of the author; **Trevor Harvey**: 'I've Been Playing with Words' © Trevor Harvey 2000, first published in *Playing with Words*, ed. Brian Moses (Longman), included by permission of the author; **J. Patrick Lewis**: 'A Parrot' © J. Patrick Lewis 2003, included by permission of the author; **George Moore**: 'Knitted Scarf Poem' © George Moore 1982, first published in the programme notes for *Over To You* (Central TV), included by permission of the author; **Peter Mortimer**: 'The Boy Who Mislaid His Vowels (inc. y) Writes a Note to His Teacher' © Peter Mortimer 2001 from *The Expanded Utter Nonsense* (IRON Press); **Brian Moses**: 'How Can I?' © Brian Moses 1995, first published in *Rice, Pie and Moses* (Macmillan), included by permission of the author; **John Rice**: 'Low Owl' © John Rice 1991, first published in *Bears Don't Like Bananas* (Hodder) included by permission of the author; **Andy Seed**: 'Hindsight' © Andy Seed 2003, first published in *Funny Poems*, compiled by Jan Dean (Scholastic), included by permission of the author; **Colin West**: 'Smith, Hacket, and Grimes' and 'Short Words' both © Colin West 1984, first published in *It's Funny When You Look At It* (Hutchinson), included by permission of the author.